# TALES OF THE TEIGN

## Chips Barber and Judy Chard

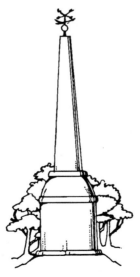

OBELISK PUBLICATIONS

## ALSO BY THE AUTHORS
Around & About the Haldon Hills, Chips Barber
The Lost City of Exeter, Chips Barber
Diary of a Dartmoor Walker, Chips Barber
The Torbay Book, Chips Barber
Diary of a Devonshire Walker, Chips Barber
The Great Little Dartmoor Book, Chips Barber
The Great Little Exeter Book, Chips Barber
The Great Little Totnes Book, Chips Barber
The DevonAir Book of Family Walks, Chips Barber
Made in Devon, Chips Barber & David FitzGerald
Dartmoor in Colour, Chips Barber
Exeter in Colour, Chips Barber
Torbay in Colour, Chips Barber
Dark and Dastardly Dartmoor, Sally and Chips Barber
Ghosts of Exeter, Sally and Chips Barber
Burgh Island and Bigbury Bay, Chips Barber & Judy Chard
Tales of the Unexplained in Devon, Judy Chard
Haunted Happenings in Devon, Judy Chard

For further details of these or any of our titles, please send SAE to
Obelisk Publications at the address below, or telephone Exeter (0392) 68556

## ACKNOWLEDGEMENTS
Many thanks to everyone who helped with materials for this book — we have tried to name names where possible, and offer our sincere apologies for anyone left out! Particular thanks to Mr W. J. Reynolds for reading the Script and making some useful suggestions!

## PLATE ACKNOWLEDGEMENTS
Chips Barber for pages 4, 6, 8, 9, 14, 15, 20, 23, 24, 25, 26, 28 and 31
Mr Norton for page 3, Silverlands for page 19
Angler's Rest for page 12 (top) Judy Chard (bottom)
Jane Reynolds for all drawings and cover pictures
Sally Barber for page 5, and for Maps on pages 7 and 16/17

*First published in 1990*
*by Obelisk Publications, 2 Church Hill, Pinhoe, Exeter, Devon,*
*Designed by Chips and Sally Barber*
*Edited and Typeset by Sally Barber*
*Printed in Great Britain by Penwell Ltd, Parkwood, Callington, Cornwall*

# TALES OF THE TEIGN

In writing this book we feel we must ask the readers' indulgence to some extent over what we can only term a kind of poetic licence—in other words some of the strange and unusual stories we write about are not strictly on the actual banks of the River Teign, but at least they have some connection, and are included because of their interest.

Every river is an individual with its own legends and mysteries, and the Teign is no exception. It starts its life in two parts, north and south. The North Teign rises in one of the wildest and most desolate—but starkly beautiful—areas of Dartmoor bog not far from Cranmere Pool beneath Whitehorse Hill. Cranmere Pool is somewhat of a contradiction

in terms and any walker visiting the area for the first time should not expect to encounter a sheet of water—it is more than likely that the 'pool' will be almost empty—or 'low tide' as wags would put in the visitors' book, the first and one of the few 'official' Dartmoor letterboxes. Obviously 'Cranmere Benjie' has been hard at work here ...

Benjamin Gayer was a rich miller and mayor of Okehampton, and when he died his ghost was condemned to drain the pool at Cranmere with a sieve. He was no fool and set his brain to solve this problem, which he did neatly by spreading a sheepskin across the bottom of the sieve and, in revenge, baling out all the water, drowning Okehampton town. Eventually he was turned into a black colt by the local parson and was ridden back to Cranmere and plunged into the pool. Since then he has haunted the area, whinnying to put the fear of God into any walkers in the area.

However, this is a land of rainfall with figures usually in excess of 1500 mm per annum. This plateau-like tableland landscape is badly drained and presents any explorers on foot with a decidedly difficult terrain, the sort it is easier to hop across rather than walk. The broad expanse of blanket bog gives rise to many rivers which includes the Taw, the East Dart and the West Okement which actually rises at Cranmere Pool.

Our friend, the Teign, starts about a mile from Cranmere and exhibits in its entire length, of about thirty miles, the disorientating habit of changing direction a great many times. It is almost as if it flows in a state of total confusion. Various geomorphological theories have been put forward to suggest that changes in the landscape have affected Dartmoor's rivers. It is believed that the Dart once used the Teign Estuary and that the Teign flowed into the Exe Estuary! No small wonder then that our river finds it difficult to make up its mind about where it is going. We will follow it step by step to make sure it arrives safely in Teignmouth.

• The rising North Teign is soon joined by the streams of Little and Great Varracombe, and reaches the first of many bridges below the ruins of Teignhead Farm, one of Britain's loneliest homesteads providing shelter for moormen. It was built in 1780 and was inhabited until 1943, when the War Office terminated the tenancy, by many colourful

characters including George Endacott, who was thrown out in 1876 for non payment of rent. Another, Jimmy Brock, frequently got paralytic drunk at the Railway Inn at Princetown and was hoisted on to his pony, only arriving safely home due to the sagacity of the animal. His wife, Mrs Brock, was an enormous woman who invited those whom she considered friends into her kitchen for cider or tea, but the visitors did have to share the room with a pig which always lay under the table!

Manga House once stood on the hill of the same name, one of the most intriguing ruins on Dartmoor. No documentary mention of the farm is made but there is a plan of the site on a map dated 1839. Local tradition says it was abandoned before Teignhead Farm was built and that would be before 1780, and was last occupied by a branch of the Endacott family.

In Eric Hemery's wonderful book, *High Dartmoor*, there is the suggestion, by a London headmaster, of a pixie in this area in 1950. This was at Manga Falls, a little further down the North Teign River, where he was sitting to rest and admire the falls. Suddenly he was spattered with small pebbles and naturally got up to investigate. He could find no one but—as one often gets on Dartmoor—he had this overwhelming feeling he was being watched and he left the area, glad to return to normality. So who would question the fact that there are still pixies on Dartmoor?

It is not uncommon for walkers, perhaps training for such gruelling events as the Ten Tors Expedition, to become 'pixie-led', a quaint moorland term for getting lost. In the barren landscape which borders the Teign in these parts it is easy to lose one's way, particularly if the cloud cover is low or a walking party is enveloped by mist. In this region of the moor the flat expanses of Gidleigh Common Mire can form quite a frightening prospect for anyone who has the misfortune to get lost when the weather is 'up to tricks' as the moor folks will say.

In the last century a Dartmoor peasant, believed to be searching the moor for lost sheep, stumbled across the body of a sailor which lay close to the point where the Walla Brook meets the North Teign River. Perhaps he had strayed from the Mariner's Way, a route sailors took between the ports of North Devon and those on the south coast in order to avoid the long sea journey around the often stormy waters of the South West peninsular. Although the details of his plight are scanty it appears he died with a serene expression on his face with his head resting gently on a bundle of linen. At his feet were found the remains of his faithful dog, both victims of the appalling weather that Dartmoor can suddenly throw up.

All the while the North Teign River is growing in volume supplemented by a great many tiny tributary streams. One flows down from the western flank of a hill which boasts a plethora of names. Shoveldon, Shuffle, Shovel or even Shuggle Down (all variations of the same name) is a system of stone rows running in a northerly direction which nineteenth-century observers described as part of a grand Druidical scheme.

In this deserted area it's odd to think that in the past it teemed with life and that the great rock of Kes Tor stands above what was once a huge settlement of early Britons, their hut circles still covering the slopes with rings of enormous blocks of stone. The cattle pounds are a reminder that wolves once hunted the area whilst the men who watched over the livestock, now lay beneath the barrows on the invariably cloudy hilltops.

Amidst all the ancient archaeological attractions is a conspicuous landmark called the Long Stone, a rough monolith of great size located about half a mile to the south of the North Teign—or half a mile north of the South Teign! When the bounds were beaten the task fell on one of the 'bounders' to climb to the top of it. For such a tricky climb the participant was given a small monetary award.

The nearby Teign-e-ver clapper bridge could also tell some tales, echoing down the years with the sounds of moormen passing over it, possibly carrying peat from off the high northern moors a few miles distant. Not far from here is a tolmen, a holed stone with a diameter of 3 feet 4 inches. Some superstitious folk believe that sufferers of arthritis or rheumatism can be cured by crawling through the dolmen in a downward direction. It may cure them, but will probably kill them as well! William Crossing misguidedly explains

it was used for mysterious purposes by the ubiquitous Druids, who seem to have spent a great deal of their time contriving puzzles for posterity.

Less romantically, the hole is made as a result of a pebble being washed into a depression in the rock, which deepens through the grinding action over the years, getting bigger and bigger.

The wild beauty of this area is still unspoilt—Teign Border country—and before we leave the uplands we must have a look at Gidleigh Tor, which has the nickname Prinsep's Folly, and is the site of a Devon house which became a folly because of its situation. It was built on the tor in 1846 by Thomas Levett Prinsep, who died before he could move in. The house was demolished some time before 1850, although no one seems to know exactly why. He had chosen the most difficult site possible, meaning it to blend in with the rocks and tors. You can still see part of the walls and a tiny roofless tower near the top of the hill—the epitome of sheer folly.

Gidleigh is a hamlet with a parish church through whose grounds a stream runs. Nearby are the remains of Gidleigh Castle, a fortified manor house built about 1300. The village takes its name from Gydda, a Danish princess and niece of King Canute. She married Earl

Godwin and became the mother of King Harold, who was said to have been born here.

Below Gidleigh is a deep, steep valley through which flows the Blackaton Brook, itself joining the River Teign a short distance above Leigh Bridge. Crossing this fast flowing little river is a bridge which, to all appearances, looks quite normal and is indeed an extremely peaceful spot, except of course on some dark nights when the silence is shattered by the noise of musket fire and sword play! It is believed this was the scene of a skirmish during the English Civil War (1642-1646) and that the opposing sides return to re-enact their conflict.

Another ghost which may be seen on this bridge, from time to time, is that of a woman who committed suicide by drowning herself in the river.

The other half of the river, the South Teign, rises just above Fernworthy Forest to the south-south-east of Teignhead Farm. In the same direction, silhouetted against the sky line exactly like a flock of sheep, are the two stone circles named Grey Wethers (a 'wether' being a castrated ram). Crossing tells the story of the innocent sheep farmer who, over a tankard of either ale or cider—probably the latter—at the Warren House Inn, was beguiled into purchasing a very reasonably priced flock of 'grey wethers'. But when he rode out later to view his purchase, he discovered they were merely lumps of granite!

Fernworthy reservoir was opened on 22nd June 1942 to help supply Newton Abbot, Torquay and Bovey Tracey. The water is held back by a dam across the valley of the South Teign. From here it is pumped to Tottiford, Trenchford and Kennick before going on to its final destination. Its one claim to fame is that it is the last all granite dam to be built on Dartmoor. Although no dwellings or farm buildings were submerged, some prehistoric retaining circles and a clapper bridge lie beneath the normal water level, and can be seen only during a drought such as in the summers of 1955, 1976 and 1989. At such times Fernworthy becomes a mecca of the multitudes with thousands of visitors flocking to see the water which isn't there! The Forestry Commission, South West Water and the Dartmoor National Park Authority have combined to provide recreational facilities for the public to enjoy. Waymarked trails through the forest can be explored from April to October whilst the three and a half mile trek around the reservoir is open all year round. The forest trails are a blessing to those who lack a sense of direction as the woods are fairly extensive and the paths numerous, so without the benefit of route marking getting lost would be a formality!

From this area comes a rather gloomy story about the franklin, or freeholder, and his wife who built their new home, from granite, on the site of an older house which had been inhabited by their family for many generations. The couple patiently awaited the arrival of their first child until in due course a son was born. But other creatures had also been hoping for just such an event. One winter's evening, when the light had nearly faded and the fire burned low, the mother slept for a moment instead of keeping watch over the cradle which held the precious baby. When she woke she heard a low laugh and thought she saw a figure in a grey cloak. To her horror she found the child had gone. The pixies had bided their time and then wreaked their revenge on the humans who had dared to quarry granite from rocks which belonged to them. The penalty was the loss of the first baby born in the house.

On a less sad note, there is a granite rock called the Heath Stone, standing close to the unclassified road which leads to the extensive Fernworthy Forest. For many years the reservoir had a warden who was also a lay preacher and could be heard all around the district preaching the Word of the Lord. The Heath Stone's virgin surface proved too great a 'temptation' for him. He decided to leave a lasting message of his beliefs on the rock by carving part of a text from St John's Gospel. He managed to chisel "Jesus said, I am the way, the truth and the light" but Dartmoor has many watchdogs, and preservationists number heavily amongst their ranks—alas he did not get to finish his quote!

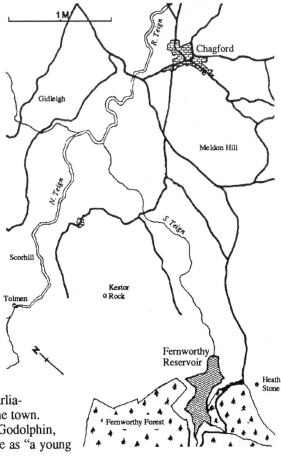

Just over two miles downstream, the North and South Teign Rivers join forces at Leigh Bridge and from there the Teign runs on down to Chagford. Here we have a feast of legends and folklore, but only room for a few.

In February 1643 Sir John Berkeley of the Royalists attacked and dispersed some Parliamentary forces quartered in the town. A romantic cavalier, Sidney Godolphin, described in books of the time as "a young gentleman of incomparable parts", aged 18, a poet and friend of Ben Johnson, was shot above the knee by a musket ball and died almost immediately. They carried him into the porch of the Three Crowns Inn where his ghost is now said to haunt the pub, many people having heard his footsteps on the stairs and in the passages.

Some people say the following story was the inspiration for R. D. Blackmore's scene in *Lorna Doone*, as he was a frequent visitor to this part of Devon. The Whiddon family were well known in Chagford for centuries. In the chancel of Chagford Church lie the remains of Mary Whiddon who, on her wedding day in October 1641, was shot at the altar by her former lover as she was about to marry someone else. On her tomb are engraved these words:-

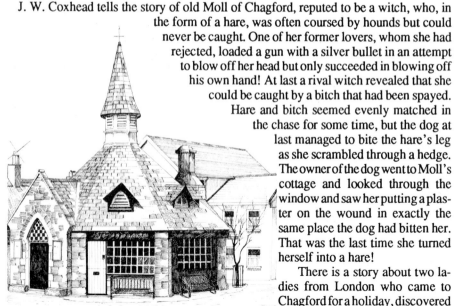

*Reader, Wouldn'st Though Know Who*
    *Here Is Laid,*
*Behold A Matron Yet A Maid*
*A Modest Looke, A Pious Heart*
*A Mart For The Better Part*
*But Drie Thine Eies Why Wilt Thou*
    *Weep*
*Such Doubtless Doe Not Die But*
    *Sleepe.*

As recently as 1971 her ghost has been seen when the daughter of the family living at Whiddon Park was to be married at the church in Chagford. On the morning of the wedding one of the guests said he saw a young woman standing in the doorway of his bedroom, dressed in an old fashioned wedding dress. As he spoke to her, she vanished.

J. W. Coxhead tells the story of old Moll of Chagford, reputed to be a witch, who, in the form of a hare, was often coursed by hounds but could never be caught. One of her former lovers, whom she had rejected, loaded a gun with a silver bullet in an attempt to blow off her head but only succeeded in blowing off his own hand! At last a rival witch revealed that she could be caught by a bitch that had been spayed. Hare and bitch seemed evenly matched in the chase for some time, but the dog at last managed to bite the hare's leg as she scrambled through a hedge. The owner of the dog went to Moll's cottage and looked through the window and saw her putting a plaster on the wound in exactly the same place the dog had bitten her. That was the last time she turned herself into a hare!

There is a story about two ladies from London who came to Chagford for a holiday, discovered a perfectly delightful cottage and thought it would make an ideal holiday home. They enquired of the owner of the cottage if they might come back later to stay awhile and it was agreed. However, when they returned there was no sign of any building, just a heap of stones and rubble—thick with brambles and nettles—was all that marked the site. It was quite obvious it had not been disturbed for years.

As you come out of Chagford, turn left onto the main A382 road, and you will soon see a turning to the right marked Shilstone and Drewsteignton. Follow this lane and opposite a private house stands a big cromlech or dolmen, said to be the only one in Dartmoor country—or indeed in Devon—which is not in a ruined condition. Even this dolmen is a restoration for it fell during a storm in 1862 and was rebuilt the same year. As it stands on private ground you must ask permission to look at it.

According to legend this monument was raised by three spinsters—not unmarried ladies, but spinners of yarn. They were on their way home from work when they saw these three great stones lying on the ground, and decided to build the dolmen, which became known as Spinsters' Rock. Crossing remarks, "It is rather humiliating to reflect that what could only be accomplished by men in the nineteenth century with the expenditure of much labour and time, was, in the 'dim old days', effected by three women one morning before breakfast."

Below Chagford the Teign wanders through some pleasant grassy meadows; it is possible to follow its banks for many miles downstream on foot away from the noise and fumes of traffic. This would have been the route of a railway running from Chagford to Dunsford Halt, if elaborate plans drawn up to join the Teign Valley line with a railway to serve the inland and popular Victorian resort of Chagford had come to fruition. But the scheme was abandoned and, of course, had it been engineered, it would have fallen in the days of the Beeching 'axe' anyway!

The waters of the Teign are diverted to fill Chagford's outdoor swimming pool, the

perfect venue for a bracing bathe. In the past the waters of the Teign powered many mills. In Chagford alone there was the beautiful Holy Street Mill which ground corn, and not far from that Yeo Mill did much the same, but from January 1893 it produced electricity, one of the earliest power plants of its type recorded. It was ingeniously used to operate all sorts of equipment associated with saw milling. At Rushford Mill, just below the swimming pool, corn was ground until 1947, outlasting the rival Sandy Park Mill, a mile or so downstream, by some 30 years. The latter has since become the Mill End Hotel which is sited beside Dogmarsh Bridge. Just up the road is the Sandy Park Inn which at one time had the (self-confessed) rudest landlord in the kingdom!

The Teign now approaches its gorge and a casual warning is offered to would-be picnickers. For some reason the geology of this area, from Sandy Park to Steps Bridge and beyond, seems to be favoured by millions of large red ants!

Castle Drogo stands above on a high spur of land sticking out spectacularly into the Teign Gorge. It is a National Trust property and is well worth a visit. The architect was the much travelled Edwin Landseer Lutyens, grandfather of politician Nicholas Ridley. Apart from the war memorial near Exeter Cathedral and the Drum Inn at Cockington near

Torquay, this great architect designed the Whitehall Cenotaph in London, the British Embassy in Washington, the government buildings in New Delhi, and also did much restoration work on places like Lindisfarne Castle. Even so, Castle Drogo was a task and a half, and Lutyens was over 20 years older by the time it was completed. Work began on the last castle to be built in England in 1910 at the instigation of Julius Drewe, a self made millionaire. He bought the glebelands in the parish of Drewsteignton and chose this most magnificent site for his castle.

Nearby, the tiny hilltop village of Drewsteignton lies close to the Teign, as its name would suggest, but it is not possible to see the river from it. However walkers can have a lot of fun negotiating the various footpaths that lead from the village towards the valley. In walking such a beautiful area it is hard to imagine that Drewsteignton could ever contain anything which could be remotely unpleasant but, according to some, it does.

In the neighbourhood of the village is a place called Bloody Corner. It is believed that a gruesome murder was committed here and, on the anniversary of this foul and dastardly deed, a thin trickle of blood can be seen flowing from below a cottage door and onto the roadway below. All this supposedly happens at midnight, which is perhaps just as well as most folk will be snugly tucked up by then and will not have to witness the scene.

Fingle Bridge is one of the most beautiful locations in Devon, a fact not only acknowledged by R. D. Blackmore, author of *Lorna Doone*, but by the thousands of visitors who come back to it time after time. The sixteenth century packhorse bridge provides access to the south bank of the river and was used by traders visiting the corn mill which once stood a little way downstream on the right hand bank, and also by those who took full advantage of the woods for fuel, for charcoal and bark.

About 1897 an astute lady from Drewsteignton, called Jessie Ashplant, noting that many visitors were 'discovering' Fingle Bridge, provided pots of tea for the thirsty folk. After some ten years she used the little pot of money that she made to invest in a modest tea shelter. At first its corrugated roof had to be covered with furze and bracken so that it would merge with the landscape but as trade went from strength to strength, a bigger and better structure followed in 1929. Today the Angler's Rest completes the transformation with its excellent restaurant and fine pub. The Price family have managed the venue for several generations. A perfect excuse to venture in to the pub is for a peek at the

wooden fish which adorn the walls. These are replicas of fish taken from the Teign and were fashioned in wood by Harry Price. He believed that it was a waste to stuff a perfectly good fish, so made an exact copy and consumed the original!

On the south side of the Teign Gorge, which runs from Castle Drogo to Steps Bridge, are a series of lofty hills and downs. Mardon Down is a fine example and stands high above the Teign. It is a popular place, on fine days, with people walking this great open area with views ranging across to Northern Dartmoor, where the Teign begins, right around towards the higher parts of Exeter. Exmoor's distant outline can be clearly seen on brighter days. Hereabouts is a menhir or large standing stone which is known as Maximajor's Grave or, as some authorities state, 'Maximager's Grave'. According to a local legend the stone is named after a giant of that name. It is probable that he lived a troubled life because if you visit the stone at midnight you may well hear the most pitiful cries or wailing coming from this stone.

Although it is not on the banks of the river itself, we must mention Great Fulford before we leave this beautiful area. This private mansion lies about two miles to the north of Mardon Down, on the opposite side of the Teign Valley. Fulfords have been in Devon

since Anglo Saxon times, occupied as farmers, aldermen, soldiers, justices of the peace etc. and the sequence of the family name has gone directly through the male line for more than seven centuries, since Richard I to the present day. Of course they haven't all been models of perfection, one named Henry, born about 1360, was accused of rioting in Chagford during the Wat Tyler rebellion when he attacked Thomas Creedy, Sergeant-at-arms and could perhaps be labelled an early hooligan?

The most fascinating story from there comes from the late Vincent Wills of Exeter and is told in full, in his own words, in *Haunted Happenings in Devon*. Briefly, his story is about a recurring dream he had as a child which always seemed intensely menacing—more of a nightmare—situated in an old crumbling house. He always woke from the dream in a bath of sweat. Many years later, when he was working in the office of a small building firm under contract to work at Great Fulford, he went to fetch one of the workmen from the house, and found himself reliving his childhood dream. He was never able to identify why he felt quite so uneasy, but when the story was related on local radio, a man rang the studio to say there had been a murder in the attic of the house—a chandelier had been fixed to fall and crush a child to death. Unfortunately this fascinating explanation has never been verified.

Vincent's cousin also had a scary moment when he saw Squire Fulford's ghost who, at 12 midnight, drives a coach with four headless horses through the village (a phenomenon which seems to haunt many of our villages).

As you leave this area the valley widens slightly below Clifford Bridge and the river flows on through green meadows and woods towards Steps Bridge. The village of Dunsford is less than half a mile away, off the main B3212 road which travels from Exeter to Moretonhampstead in a most tortuous fashion. It is a quiet, moorland edge village with a good community spirit. Many of its working population commute to Exeter and return each night to enjoy the relative peace and quiet that life in the Teign Valley offers. The original route from Exeter to Moreton passed through the village and instead of crossing Steps Bridge made its way along the Boyland Road to cross the Teign upstream at Clifford Bridge.

Whilst driving or walking around these lanes it may well be worth keeping a wary eye out for a pair of ghosts who will be easily identified. These two spirits are a pair of lovers who discovered that the course of true love never runs smooth. Whilst out for a romantic jaunt one summer's evening they quarrelled, in the heat of the moment the young man strangled his loved one—using a stocking that she had been knitting to commit the murderous deed. This was produced as evidence at his trial and he was convicted of murder and hanged. However that was not the end of the story for the sweethearts have been seen on numerous occasions, sitting peacefully together on a stile—with the young girl continuing with the knitting that she never finished, nor ever will!

Steps Bridge, the closest point on the Teign to Dunsford, is a place where multitudes of visitors flock in the Spring, specifically to admire the carpets of daffodils which clothe

the woods here. This part of the valley is a nature reserve and, if you are quiet and choose your time when others are not around, you will see a wealth of wildlife. There are strategically placed information boards to educate visitors about all the flora and fauna found in the neighbourhood.

The waterfall at Steps Bridge is man made but not solely for the purpose of creating a beauty spot. Iron Mills manufactured edge tools like spades and scythes. In order to operate their machinery, which included tilt hammers and grind stones, a waterwheel was necessary. To turn the waterwheel a leat was required and to supply the leat a waterfall was necessary—to create a sufficient head of water. To control the flow of water, sluice gates were installed beside Steps Bridge.

The Teign soon starts to turn away from its general eastward course in favour of a more southerly direction. In a few miles it is joined by the route of the former Teign Valley Railway. This railway is described in more detail in *Around and About the Haldon Hills.*

Its main function was to serve the many mines and quarries of the Teign Valley. None of the stations which bore the names of Christow, Dunsford, Longdown or Chudleigh were anywhere near the villages so, as people began to acquire their own vehicles, the passenger trade tailed off and the line closed in 1958. Since then Christow Station has been cleverly landscaped and adapted.

The Sheldon Centre was started by the Rev. Geoffrey Fraser and has accommodated many young people in its time. The centre has an impressive outdoor theatre which puts on a variety of entertainments on summer evenings. Its present warden, Rev. Carl Lee, is a man of many parts who has enthusiastically spread the Word of the Lord not only at Sheldon, but also through the airwaves of a local radio station. It might be considered a minor miracle that Harry Secombe should feature Sheldon on his *Highway* programme about Crediton as this is many miles to the north and further away than Exeter!

There are many tiny villages and hamlets tucked into tributary valleys like Doddiscombsleigh, where stands the Nobody Inn, an unusual name said to arise from several possible reasons. One variation tells how the landlord was so often away spending his time drinking in Newton Abbot, or visiting its famous market, that there was 'nobody in' at the pub and people had to serve themselves. We should be so lucky! Another story relates that one of the landlords was so fond of the inn that even in death he refused to leave it. At his funeral people became suspicious as his coffin was so light. They opened it and found 'no body in' it, the suggestion being that he was buried at the pub instead. Perhaps the foundation of this tale is based on a true story as told to us by Bill Rowland of Ide. His brother-in-law, Fred, was a close friend of Dick Lewis, landlord of the New Inn at Doddiscombsleigh. Mr Lewis was employed in the local barytes mines and was admitted to the Royal Devon and Exeter Hospital in Exeter suffering with silicosis. Sadly he died and was buried in the village. However, a few days after his burial his widow was roused at 2 a.m. and informed that the grave was to be opened as they had buried the wrong body. Mrs

Lewis left the inn shortly afterwards and the pub was renamed the Nobody Inn. Whether this was meant to be a sick joke or an accidental choice of name is not known for sure.

Ashton is another lovely little village in its own tributary valley on the east side of the Teign, a mile to the south of Doddiscombsleigh. Here we find Place Barton, an estate which belonged to the Chudleigh family, Lords of the Manor of Ashton from 1320-1745, whose most notorious member must have been Elizabeth Chudleigh. She was born at Harford in the Erme valley in 1720. Incredibly beautiful, she caught the eye of many important and influential people including William Pulteney, the Earl of Bath, who secured for her a position as Maid of Honour to the Princess of Wales at a favourable salary. George II was greatly taken with Elizabeth, showering her with gifts, giving her mother the post of housekeeper at Windsor, and organising a masquerade ball in Elizabeth's honour. However she blotted her copybook by appearing at the masquerade dressed—or rather undressed—as Iphigenia. The Princess of Wales was not amused.

On the spur of the moment, Elizabeth had married a naval lieutenant, Augustus John Hervey at Winchester in 1744, but she kept it a secret as she did not want to lose her income. Regretting her impulsive action, she later destroyed the evidence of the union. Then the husband she didn't wish to be connected with became Earl of Bristol, and was said to be on his death bed. Seeing an opportunity to gain a title, she attempted to have the marriage record restored. However, as her husband didn't oblige her by dying, she moved on to other opportunities. Elizabeth 'married' the Duke of Kingston, from whom she inherited a vast fortune on his death, but the Duke's nephew instigated a trial to prove bigamy. She was found guilty, but claimed Benefit of a Peer and was absolved from prison. She then left England and the Czarina Catherine made her welcome in Russia, where she bought a mansion near St Petersburg which she named Chudleigh. She died in Paris in 1788 asking to be buried at Chudleigh in Devon. A large sum of money had been set aside for a monument to be erected at Chudleigh church, but her wishes were never fulfilled.

Admiral Edward Pellew, the first Viscount Exmouth, bought Canonteign estate, on the western side of the Teign Valley, early in the nineteenth century. His wife was a lady of strong character, well able to manage his affairs during his long absences at sea. She built

Canonteign House and landscaped the extraordinary gorge with its waterfall, said to be the highest in the country. Splashing and foaming as it flows from black rocks high above Canonteign House, it is a breathtaking sight you can see for yourself as the present Viscount has opened the falls and the farm park to the public.

Drews Spinsters Rock X

Castle Drogo

Sandy Park X

Most fascinating of all perhaps is that fact that it wasn't until 1985 that anyone had set foot in this beautiful corner of the estate for more than 150 years. When Paul Exmouth started to cut back the tangle of bushes and brambles, he realised what lay behind the rock which hangs over a secret garden full of wild flowers and ferns; he crawled 100 yards through the undergrowth and found another lake and an old iron mine, Shuttamoor, with all the adits still in existence and a dam where he planned to fix a sluice gate.

Gidleigh X

N. Teign

Tolmen X

Kestor X Rock

Chagford X

Teignhead Farm X

S. Teign

Fernworthy Reservoir

B3212

When asked if Canonteign is haunted, the Viscount replied that when he was a child he used to hear odd sounds. His grandfather said there was definitely a ghost, although he didn't actually describe it, but doors would open and then slam for no reason. The odd part is that when he died in 1970 it all stopped.

There is a story that a local farmer did very well out of the Civil War thanks to Doctor Thomas Clifford, who was forced to flee from a surprise attack on the house in Bovey Tracey where he was playing cards with other Royalists. It is said the Cavaliers owed their escape to the greed of the Parliamentary soldiers because as they fled, someone threw a handful of gold coins out of the window at the feet of the soldiers, who naturally stopped to pick them up, thus awarding the escaping Royalists a few precious moments. As the Doctor ran, and his pursuers began to draw close, he threw a bag of coins over the hedge. It fell into a lime kiln and was found the next morning by the local farmer who spent the money wisely, gradually building up a prosperous business!

Many Civil War battles raged back and forth around this area and there is a legend that there is still undiscovered treasure here. This belonged to John Cann, a Royalist who, concealing himself from the Roundheads, hid for a time by the Bottor Rocks near Hennock. He secreted his treasure somewhere in the vicinity. Eventually he was tracked down by bloodhounds and taken out and hanged. Meanwhile a blue flame is said to hover sometimes over the place where the teasure is hidden. More prosaically this could be something to do with the old copper mines in the area.

Throughout the entire length of the Teign there are the remains of mines and quarries but the area from Bridford down to Hennock has more than its fair share. At Bridford barytes were mined and then crushed to a fine powder for use in paint manufacture, as a paper filler or for other items. Mining at Bridford ceased in 1956 which was not long past its heyday years of 1940 when 21,000 tons were produced.

Great Rock Mine, near Hennock, produced micaceous haematite from 1902 to 1970. It was used in paint manufacture and its qualities were particularly valued for protecting

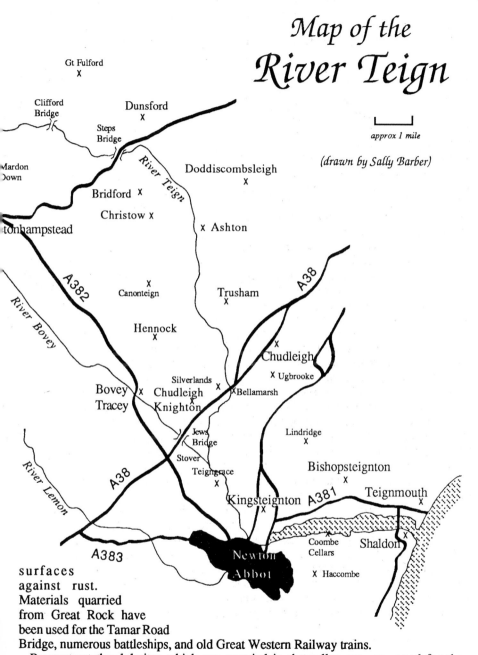

# Map of the
# River Teign

Gt Fulford
X

approx 1 mile

*(drawn by Sally Barber)*

Clifford
Bridge

Dunsford
X

Steps
Bridge

Mardon
Down

River Teign

Doddiscombsleigh
X

Bridford X

Christow X

tonhampstead

X Ashton

River Bovey

A382

X
Canonteign

Trusham
X

A38

Hennock
X

Silverlands
X

X
Chudleigh

X Ugbrooke

Bovey
Tracey

X Chudleigh
Knighton
X

XBellamarsh

River Lemon

Jews
Bridge

Lindridge
X

A38

Stover

Teigngrace
X

Bishopsteignton
X

A381

Teignmouth
X

Kingsteignton
X

A383

Newton
Abbot

Coombe
Cellars

Shaldon

X Haccombe

surfaces
against rust.
Materials quarried
from Great Rock have
been used for the Tamar Road
Bridge, numerous battleships, and old Great Western Railway trains.

By contrast the dolerites which are quarried in the valley are very good for the construction of road surfaces and you would be amazed how far afield you could drive over a little bit of the Teign Valley!

17

Several small streams rise on the western flanks of Haldon to wend their way down to the Teign. In one steep combe is the quiet village of Trusham. Those of you who have read *Tales of the Unexplained in Devon* will no doubt recall the strange story of the shining silver cross at Sherford Church near Kingsbridge. Trusham also once had an inexplicable vision in an old house which had a partition at the end of a large room to form a cupboard. Occasionally, an extremely bright golden light would emanate from the cupboard door. There was no logical explanation. As the cupboard was extremely damp, to give it more ventilation, the partitioning panel was removed and the weird and wonderful light or aura was not witnessed again. This strange occurrence was noted just after the First World War and followed the death of a young man who hanged himself from a nearby ash tree. It is not known whether the two incidents are connected, but the ghost of the man has been seen near the ash tree on various occasions.

Trusham also has another strange phenomena—a black patch which exists in one of the lanes near the village. People coming upon it at night have felt an experience akin to running into a force field, or at least something more solid than thin air. No apparent interpretation of such a weird occurrence has been given to our knowledge.

It used to be reckoned that the best view of the Teign Valley was to be had from the public conveniences at the Palk Arms in Hennock, a loo with a view! However those of us who have walked the hills around the Teign Valley hill top village of Hennock will no doubt give other locations as better vantage points. Getting to such places in the past has proved a problem. In snowy, wintry weather the steep lanes can become impassable, snow drifts being several feet deep, but even at other times when the weather has been fair there

have been problems for Hennock-bound motorists. Between Pitt Hill and the village there have been three separate bicycle accidents. In all three cases the cyclists lived to tell the tale that there was a spectre running alongside the road wildly gesticulating and waving about its arms so much that it caused them to fall off. Unfortunately no other details have come to light on these peculiar happenings.

Just outside the small town centre of Bovey Tracey is a house where the owners installed an old staircase which had been discarded from the original Buckfast Abbey. On the backs of some of the treads the carved names and initials of monks were discovered. These marks were from centuries past but the removal of their beloved staircase was probably instrumental in stirring the monks into action; every evening, at about the same time, they could be clearly seen passing up and down the stairs. The residents, who were initially taken aback by these manifestations, became accustomed to them as there was no malevolence or bad vibrations emanating from the spooks—the children of the house would even delay their bed times so that the ghostly monks would come and stand beside them. However the media heard of the haunted happenings and their presence was deemed menacing so that the family had little alternative but to call in a priest to exorcise the benign ghostly monks.

The family who own Silverlands is well used to living with ghosts. They spent five years exhibiting their famous model, Silvers Circus, in the Spanish Barn at Torre Abbey in Torquay which is one of the most well-known haunted buildings in the West Country.

However, once they moved to Stokelake House at Chudleigh and opened it as the popular family attraction, Silverlands, they thought they had left ghosts and eerie experiences behind them. But not so. The rambling old mansion house had been left empty and derelict for many years and, as soon as the work of renovation began, stories came to them from locals and neighbours. Apparently, long ago, a groom had hung himself in the stable block which is now part of the main restaurant, and his ghost was said to haunt that wing of the building. Also there was much talk of a ghostly butler who welcomed guests at the front door then vanished.

Intrigued, the family invited a clairvoyant friend to dinner in the hope that she might be able to shed some light on the mysteries. Without any prompting from them she detected an unhappy presence in the former stable area. Also, much to their surprise, she informed them that the spirit of a very pleasant lady was hovering about the main staircase, and that she seemed very happy that the old house was being restored and used once more. Then, during the months of restoration, there was a progression of small but unexplained incidents: tools disappeared and reappeared; children's voices were heard late at night but searches of the house revealed nothing; lights were repeatedly found switched on in unused rooms; pork pies would regularly vanish from the kitchen fridge only to reappear in the most unlikely places; and, on several occasions, a white-coated figure was seen wandering the corridors by members of the family, including the children.

Since Silverlands has been open to the public there have been less unexplained incidents although the sightings of the white-coated figure have continued. But the family has grown used to living with the ghosts and their strange ways.

From now on road and river run side by side as far as Chudleigh bridge. The Teign doesn't actually run through the village itself, but a tributary, the Katebrook or Kidbrook, flows through a steeply wooded glen to join the river near the site of the old Chudleigh station, which is now covered over by the A38 road.

Chudleigh Rocks rise high above this gorge and consist of cliffs of limestone, honeycombed with caves and an inner cul-de-sac which is known as Pixies' Parlour. In Victorian times Chudleigh women tied their babies to their cots to prevent their being whisked off as changelings by the pixies.

Some famous mountaineers have been known to scale these Rocks in preparation for some of the most difficult climbs on this planet. Other adventurers prefer to explore Chudleigh Cavern where prehistoric man once lived. Pottery, charcoal and flint implements have been found in the caves which are called such delightful names as Toad's Penance, Belfry, Bones' Chamber and Pope's Head with a smaller cave rather unromantically called Cow Cave!

This beautiful glen holds another story about the little people. Near here lived a gamekeeper, his wife and two small children. One morning the eldest child wandered off and was reported missing. Everyone rallied round in the search, even blood-hounds were brought in, but there was no sign of her. She was eventually discovered by two young men who had been gathering hazel nuts in the area. She was completely naked, but quite normal and happy and unhurt and despite the length of time she was missing, she wasn't at all hungry. The young men said she was "sitting on a bank, playing with her toes!" To the superstitious locals it was obvious the pixies had taken the original child but why they returned such a hearty specimen in exchange is not clear.

Incidentally, there are only two things pixies fear—holy water and the sound of church bells, but if you become pixie-led, turn your coat inside out and this will send them away.

Chudleigh was almost entirely destroyed by fire in 1807, the compact layout of the town being its downfall. Just when people thought they had the flames under control, a barrel of gun-powder exploded and the town was razed to the ground. Money was raised in many ways, but none more so than by the direct influence of Lord Clifford, and in appreciation Mill Lane was renamed Clifford Street.

In the fourteenth century Bishop Edmund Lacey chose Chudleigh for his summer vacation, staying at the monastery, parts of which can still be seen. The Bishop Lacy pub was the only building left intact after the fire. The Inn is said to be haunted by a cloaked figure and some years ago a past landlord spoke to a man who came into the bar just at closing time. However the figure ignored him and headed up the stairs. Naturally the landlord followed him, and met his wife coming down. No one had passed her!

One of the main attractions in this area is Ugbrooke. Although the house was first mentioned in 1280, the property goes back to 1080. Daniel Lyson introduced it thus: "This novel house is descended from Sir Clifford, younger brother of Thomas Lord Clifford, ancestor of the Earls of Cumberland and of course the Fair Rosamund who was the mistress of Henry II." The house holds many priceless portraits by such people as Lely, du Cros and Opie, and some magnificent embroideries dating back to the sixteenth century. Amongst these is a silk embroidered four poster bed hanging which was worked by the widow of the ninth Duke of Norfolk around 1720, legend having it that she took 17 years to complete the work.

In the park there is a grove of beech trees known as Dryden's Walk, named after a frequent visitor to Ugbrooke who was also a close friend of the first Lord Clifford. It is said that he completed his translation of Virgil here. At the top end of the park there is a lovely view from the earthwork known as Castle Dyke, which was probably an Iron Age fort, one of many found along the Teign.

In the valley below, the Teign twists its way past the edge of Chudleigh Knighton to cross under the A38, the main Exeter to Plymouth highway. In 1822 a new coaching route entered Chudleigh from the Exeter direction, and this eventually became the A38. At this location there was once a mill called Bellamarsh Mill where, in 1795, there was a riot. For weeks country folk had suffered from acute food shortages caused largely by the Napoleonic Wars. There was a suspicion that millers were stockpiling grain in order to make more than a little 'bread' for themselves. Needless to say an unruly mob approached Bellamarsh Mill with the intention of taking some much needed grain. Among the throng was a local lad called Thomas Campion who was a blacksmith by profession. Thomas was in a state of great excitement, no doubt worked up by the passion which the crowd had generated. He attached a red handkerchief to a post, a minor enough deed but one which drew attention to him. The authorities interpreted this gesture as that as one of a leader and Thomas was duly charged with inciting and leading the uprising.

Despite his good reputation, and despite many protestations, he was found guilty at the court in Exeter. Intending to deter further rioting, the judicial system took full advantage of its power and sentenced poor Thomas to death. On Thursday, 6th August 1795 he was escorted back to Bellamarsh by soldiers from the 25th Regiment of Light Dragoons. On the gibbet he declared to the gathered assembly that he had been forced to join the riot. His hanging was the last public execution in Devon.

Below Bellamarsh the Teign enters clay country, a land cratered by numerous pits—some empty and abandoned, apart from a wealth of wildlife, others a scene of great human activity. The River Bovey, a major tributary of the Teign, joins forces a mile south of the A38 and traffic on the main road thunders over the Bovey at Jews Bridge. The bridge marks the point when the parish boundary of Bovey Tracey meets Teigngrace and possibly takes its name from a Jewish peddler who is thought to have been murdered here. In times past, long before the Turbo Age, when the pace of life was more sedate, this was a place that many locals avoided at all costs. Servants from the impressively grand Stover House, about a mile to the south, actually refused to cross this bridge as it was thought that the peddler comes back to haunt the spot.

In more recent times a lady was riding her bike home from a W.I. meeting when, as she reached the stone bridge, she saw something which seemed to be surrounded by a kind of glow. The 'thing' waved its arms and tried to jump in front of her. She arrived home very upset and when her son went out on his motor bike to investigate he had the same experience.

It is said that all old bridges are haunted because of the human sacrifices made on the original sites, which in turn had been made to placate the river gods who didn't like their domain being invaded.

Just over a mile from this spot, towards Bovey Tracey, there was once a most unusual feature, a haunted gate! People returning along the lane at night often saw the figure of a man chained to the wooden gate which led into a grassy field. People were so spooked by the regularity of sighting this poor, shackled man who was obviously distressed, that they took to making elaborate detours so they did not have to pass the spot. The apparition was eventually removed, not by a priest performing an exorcism but by the farmer installing a different type of gate. Since the mid 1950s no further sighting has been reported.

Over twenty years ago, Clare Taylor and her husband bought Ventiford Farm and one late September evening, with her son, David, was at the house cleaning the chimneys prior to moving in. In the room which at one time had been the bar of the Union Inn, they suddenly both stopped working. David turned to her and said he thought there was someone there. Although she admitted to having experienced a sudden chill, she felt a bit silly and said that all the doors were open and the lights on, and yet they both felt sure someone was standing near them. She wasn't frightened, made some teasing remark, and went on working. They then noticed the smell of pipe tobacco which Clare knew the name for—'Battle Axe'—as her grandfather always used to smoke it.

The couple intended to use this particular room as their bedroom and made it really cosy. They moved in and it was about 2 a.m. one March morning when she woke up to find her husband awake too and complaining of the cold. She smelt the tobacco again. This happened three times until they eventually moved upstairs.

The following November her daughter came to stay to have her second baby. A week after the birth she heard a noise at about 2.30 a.m. She went downstairs to find her daughter standing white and trembling in the doorway of the room. She had just seen a dark figure, a man dressed like a Roundhead, pass right through the room! Some weeks later Paul, her little son aged two, was playing in this room and said he had been talking to 'A nice lady'. She had gone through the sitting room door while it was shut!

The following Spring, Clare again woke up at two in the morning and heard a lovely lilting voice singing. She crept out of bed to see if it was the children. They were both fast asleep. She has since heard the voice many times. The old man with the pipe often visited them in the other room at Ventiford when they were sitting and watching television. David would look at her and they both knew they were smelling the tobacco.

On the right hand side of of the Ventiford Brook you can see what remains of the Ventiford Basin, the end of the Stover Canal, where the barges turned round to reload.

Stover House itself is said to be haunted—many of the pupils who have been boarders there have told of the dormitories having ghosts. And of course there is the famous story of the phantom fox at Stover ...

Stover House was once the home of John Seymour, Duke of Somerset, who was a great fox hunting fanatic, and bred these animals simply to hunt them—the fox pens can still be seen at the back of the school, rather like dungeons. The Duke bred one particular fox that was to become known for its evasive tactics and the downfall of many so-called first-class huntsmen. No one could outwit it and it became a legend in its day. This animal has been dead for over 100 years but its ghost has often been seen sitting on the wall on the perimeter of the house, on the main road opposite the Golf course. It flings itself into the air in front of passing motorists, landing on the bonnet of the car, and some people have actually felt the impact. Then it vanishes immediately to reappear on the same spot on the wall. Too late to in-

clude in *Haunted Happenings in Devon*, there was a piece in the local paper telling of a motor accident near the entrance to Stover Golf Club. A fox had jumped from the wall of the school on to a car bonnet and in swerving to avoid it the driver had hit the bank. Fortunately no one was hurt and the fox too seemed none the worse for it had returned to sit on the wall!

The Teign flows on, but somewhat mysteriously, although it is the major flow through these lowlands, the area is known as The Bovey Basin. On both sides of the river great craters appear which are the important ball clay quarries of this basin. Kingsteignton's livelihood has depended on this industry for a considerable time and the many mines and quarries have given Kingsteignton a somewhat industrial appearance.

Despite this Kingsteignton has many redeeming features and amongst them are some unusual traditions and customs. The Fairwater was an important leat which provided power to several mills. For some strange reason this man-made watercourse was so revered by local folk that to enable a person to claim the status of a 'Teigntonian' it appears that they had to fall in this stream or deliberately contrive to fall into it. The origination of Kingsteignton's famous Ram Roasting Fair is also attributable to the leat and its water, or should we say the lack of it?

Legend has it that centuries before the thinning of the Ozone layer was discovered, and blamed for every freak weather condition, there was an enduring drought in these parts. So acute was the shortage of water that there was not even enough to baptise a baby. However on the advice of a wise woman, possibly a white witch, the villagers offered up a sacrifice to appease the Rain Gods. A ram lamb was duly butchered in the parched and dried up course of the leat. And lo! the rains came and the spring sprung to replenish the leat. The superstitious locals were convinced of the success of the sacrifice and from that day on the Ram Roast has been held to maintain the water supply. It is likely that this particular legend is not too far from the truth. The all important leat served many functions and periodically had to be cleaned out. Traditionally it was

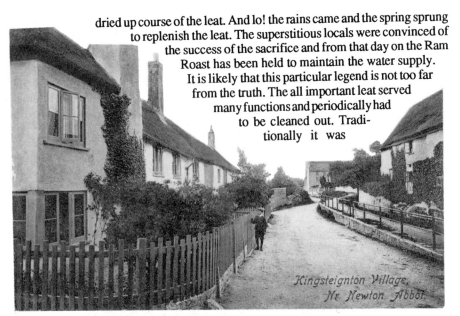

*Kingsteignton Village, Nr Newton Abbot*

turned off on Whit Sunday and all the accumulated dirt and debris was removed the next day. Prior to its ritual demise the ram was taken out to surrounding villages like Ideford and Bishopsteignton, a public appearance it performed somewhat sheepishly! On the Tuesday it was killed in the morning ready for roasting later in the day. With the Ram Roast went a whole host of activities with many sports events and numerous dances of various types taking place to complete an often raucous revel. Kingsteignton folk are often known as 'Ramroasters'.

The river flows on through Kingsteignton and eventually into the estuary after it has been joined by the Aller Brook which passes close to Forde House. Mr J. Taylor was caretaker here for a long time and he recalls an old and friendly ghost. But there seems

to have been another one, more restless, reported by a Mrs Latremouille who was once employed by a Mr and Mrs Hall at Forde House. During her term of employment in the 1930s, a young lady (a friend of Mr Hall junior) died at the house. Her body was removed in the early hours of the morning but no explanation of her death was given. Since that time, many people claim to have seen a ghostly figure on the stairs and at the same time felt intense cold and an atmosphere of unease and discomfort. Mrs Latremouille revisited the house later and sat in a chair at the bottom of the stairs, and she had the feeling of being watched by the young lady who had died. She is convinced this is the reason the house changed hands so often and was left empty for long periods before the Council took it over.

In December 1963 there was a great deal in the press about Aller House, which had been converted into flats, not far from the Barn Owl restaurant. A young couple, who had recently moved in, found their furniture being moved around, the radio switched itself either on or off, heavy footsteps were heard and a white mist was seen moving through the flat. All they could discover about the past was a suicide which had taken place about 50 years before. Originally the house belonged to the Devon Hide and Skin Co. and their manager, Albert Victor Judd committed suicide. Many people have felt some kind of presence, including Carol and John Durston, who called in the local parson, Gordon Langford, who himself said he could feel an evil presence. Eventually the Bishop of Exeter, Dr. Mortimer, was consulted and visited Aller House. As he started his usual blessing there was a notable drop in temperature, however he blessed the house and the atmosphere lightened and cleared. But a few days later the people in the next flat found themselves landed with the ghost of a young man dressed in Edwardian clothes! However he caused them no trouble so they left him in peace. Not long after the house was abandoned and demolished, probably because no one would live there.

On the River Lemon, a tributary of the Teign, stands Bradley Manor, a mediaeval manor house said to be one the finest of its kind in Devon. It too, has a ghost. Mrs Woolner, the present owner, recalls how one summer an elderly lady came to see the house. She was interested because her family had lived in the neighbourhood. When she was shown the site of the former courtyard, or triangle, west of the Great Hall, she said that was where the stables had been. She went on to recount how her grandmother had been in service at Bradley Manor and was told the stables were haunted by the ghost of a young man, a son of the house, who had been killed out riding and ever after haunted the stables to which his horse had returned. (Curiously a bridge crossing the River Lemon is known as Ghosts Bridge!) Another possible explanation, given by Theo Brown, is that the ghost is of Gilbert, the twin brother of the man killed, who is unaccounted for after the age of twenty five. A member of the family committed suicide about that time and was buried at Yarde's Cross near Shinner's Bridge in Totnes. Perhaps this also produced a ghost, and many people have heard a horse galloping through Bradley woods at the height of a storm—sensible, prosaic people such as a solicitor's wife who lives nearby.

A one time rector of Teign-grace, the Rev. Gilbert Yarde, was battered to death by his former gardener, John Greenslade, whilst walking along the road from Teigngrace to Whiteway. The man had previously asked the Reverend for a reference before changing his job and Rev. Yarde gave him one in Latin. On applying for various jobs, Greenslade noticed prospective employers visibly changed in their attitude to him directly they read the reference. He set about getting it translated and discovered it read: "Gone from me and fit for no man." At this he was so incensed he killed the rector and stole his money and gold watch. He might have gotten away with it, but one night, in his cups, he showed the watch to a mate. He was tried, found guilty of the murder and, on 18th August 1782, hanged on the gibbet near Lindridge on Little Haldon. His ghost still wanders the area.

In about 1822 the River Teign was an extremely busy marine thoroughfare due to the trade in china clay and granite. Also going about their business were the busy small passenger boats which took shoppers to Newton Abbot market and shops at least twice a day. Mary Heath plied this trade or service for many years until her death in 1863 but she was best noted for running her boat aground and constantly missing the tides in her efforts to please customers—many of whom wandered about the town and arrived late for departure. When Mary ran aground her language could be heard down the entire length of the river, no doubt making even the clay bargees blush at times. Reports over the years have been made, by complete strangers to the area, of a deep female voice cursing the sea and the tides from the mud banks opposite, where the sewage works now stand. In 1973 one person also saw a woman's figure about the same time shouts were heard. One wonders if poor Mary Heath is doomed to remain forever on these banks.

If Mary's bad language, no doubt justifiable, is still borne on the winds that blow over the Teign Estuary it is likely the sounds would be drowned by the incessant traffic flow that uses the Newton Abbot by-pass. Seen from below, the stilt-like symmetry of this modern road bridge, which was built in the mid 1970s, is most impressive.

On the north bank is the Passage House Inn, a large, fashionable pub ideally located for its estuary views. Adjacent to it once was the small hamlet of Hackney which stood on the banks of the Hackney, or as some people were wont to say, the Kingsteignton Canal. This watercourse, of less than half a mile in length, was constructed to enable clay barges to enter the Teign Estuary. The clay was carried on barges known as lighters and the lightermen who shipped the clay lived in cottages near this small canal on the edge of Hackney Marshes. They were a tough lot, and had to be, as the nature of the work of shifting vast amounts of clay, with very basic equipment, demanded great strength. However many lightermen were also hard drinkers and a certain bravado accompanied their drinking exploits. Accidents on the canal were commonplace and police records reveal that the 'demon drink' was deemed responsible for several drownings.

Perhaps though the lightermen's preference of beer to water was due to the accessibility of the former. The alehouse was nearby, but to fetch drinking water meant getting into a rowing boat and crossing the Teign to collect from the supply beyond the railway bridge.

There used to be an event called the Hackney Regatta which was held annually. Apart from the traditional goings on there was also a dubious game when locals had to chase a duck around the Marshes, something which the RSPB might take a dim view of in these more enlightened times!

Teignbridge District Council, however, should be congratulated on their efforts to instigate what most folk might call a long distance walk—but most long distance walkers would call a doddle! 'The Templer Way' is a walking route of about 15 miles which begins at Haytor Quarries and attempts to follow the Haytor Granite Tramway, the Stover Canal and the Teign Estuary in its bid to link Haytor on Dartmoor to Teignmouth with a continuous path. The route derives its name from James Templer who built the Stover Canal in 1792 and his son, George, who built the tramway in 1820. If you start at Haytor it is primarily a downhill route and the estuary section is best attempted at low tide as parts of the path become submerged at high tide. The alternative road route is harder on the feet and potentially dangerous as much traffic passes along it particularly in the summer. Teignmouth is the natural end to the walk because the granites of Haytor which have been used in such edifices as London Bridge, the Eddystone Lighthouse, Nelson's Column and the British Museum and the various ball clays of the Bovey Basin were all exported though this port. Teignbridge D.C. have produced some excellent leaflets and literature about this project and also organise various trips and adventures to explore the area.

Bishopsteignton stands on the left bank of the Teign and near here is Lindridge Park, home of the Lindridge Buddha, said to be responsible for the destruction of the once magnificent house. A more detailed history of Lindridge is told in *Tales of the Unexplained*. The Lindridge Buddha was brought to the estate by a member of the Templar family, who had connections in the far east, and it had been prophesied that if it was moved from its place below the terrace, the mansion would be destroyed by fire. After many changes of ownership the property was bought in 1962 by Mr and Mrs Brady who restored the house, the Italian, and Water Gardens to their original beauty, but they made one terrible mistake—they moved the Buddha from its place on the terrace. They were about to open the house to the public when, on the night of 25th April 1963, the house caught fire and was completely destroyed, the worst fire in Devon for over a decade. In spite of minute investigations, no logical explanation could be found for the fire. A retired Post Office worker told how he took a phone call from a man about the fire when he was on duty in the exchange—but the caller rang off before he could get his name. The brochure which was produced for the big opening states: " ... this fine and historic house was opened to the public at Easter 1963 ..." They had jumped the gun. There was no house to open.

The hamlet of Haccombe lies in a sheltered combe on the south side of the estuary, it consists mainly of occupied farms and a mansion but also one of the most perfect early English churches in existence, built by Sir Stephen de Haccombe when he returned from the Crusades in 1233. But our interest here is not in all the fascinating features of the church itself, but in one half and one whole horseshoe nailed to the outside of the south door. In the words of a nineteenth century ballad, they are said to record a wager made between a Carew of Haccombe and a Champernowne of Dartington as to whom could swim his horse the furthest into the sea. Both men ventured far out when Champernowne's horse collapsed under him and he called out for help. Carew immediately went to him and brought him safely to land on his own gallantly struggling, but exhausted, horse. Carew then rode home to Haccombe and nailed his horse's shoes to the church door—there are traces of the two other shoes which show the four having been placed in the form of a cross. The horse was put out to grass, and with his shoes now off he could put his hooves up for a well earned rest. He became a family pet, never doing another day's work.

The ballad was written long after the event, and as the nailing of horseshoes on the door was also an old charm against witches, perhaps superstition rather than fact inspired the ballad. Certainly when standing in the churchyard at Haccombe it really does not feel haunted despite its age, remoteness, and the well-stocked charnel house in the crypt.

Coombe Cellars is a name to be conjured with for it was the central place for smuggling in the area, but that is a whole story on its own and here we are concerned with the ghost. In 1968 a girl called Margaret Marshall was a barmaid at the pub. She suffered from terrible nightmares and awoke each night crying out that she was being strangled, and she

was certain her bedroom was haunted. Eventually it got so bad she went to the doctor for sleeping pills. No one took her seriously until the proprietor of the inn, Jim Harvey, went to a sale. He bought some old bits and pieces, and among them was a painting of a woman being strangled. By the dress and furniture it must have been dated a hundred years before, and showed a burglar, disturbed when he had broken into a bedroom, strangling the occupant. The picture and its inscription showed it was the room in which Margaret slept!

The following fascinating story is told in a leaflet on a wall in the Coombe Cellars Inn, displayed together with a minute piece of cork:

"For the past 300 years a fine old cork tree has flourished in the village of Combeinteignhead and has surrounded itself with a mysterious power to bring good luck to those observing certain rituals dating back to the time of the Great Plague of London in 1665. At that time people came from all parts of the country to walk around the tree three times and, as they walked, to make a wish which invariably materialised. Some came for better health, some for better fortune and others for a wife or husband as the case may be. It was said that few were disappointed. As its powers became more widely known, many people suffering from ill health but unable to make the journey to South Devon, wrote asking for a piece of the cork from its bark in order that they might walk round it three times in their own home. Others wrote asking for a piece of cork in the hope that it would bring fortune in its wake which, judging by the reports, appears to have been very satisfactory. Whatever one may think of charms and lucky omens the fact remains that this fine old tree has been the means of bringing amazing luck to those possessing a piece of its cork. The legend runs:

*Fortune favours those who see*
*More in me than just a tree*
*Take my cork*
*And three times walk*
*Round my girth for all to see.*

How such a wonderful old tree came to grow in its unusual setting, weathering the storms of hundreds of years, remains a mystery, particularly in view of its present robust and healthy condition. It is hoped that it will flourish and yield its lucky cork to future generations as in the past."

So, did the tree really exist? The relief manager, Mr Pearce, stated that he believed the whole story was something of a hoax which made a considerable amount of money for its perpetrator. However, local historian John Thorne says that a cork tree did exist, not far from Coombe Cellars, but was not as ancient as everyone was led to believe! A healthy bit of business was originated from the supposed magical qualities of the tree with misguided people coming from far and wide, even America, to perform the ritual or collect a small piece for themselves. Every day the owner of the tree collected a phenomenal amount of post, including cheques, from the local Post Office. Sadly the tree suffered from so much plundering that it died. However, unlike the tree, the business continued and thrived!

There was a certain Captain Rotham of Teignmouth, a smuggler, who on dark moonless nights would stand on the shore and wait for

a signal from the cliffs above which would tell him it was safe to land his cargo of brandy. He would be met on the beach by some farm workers from Stokeinteignhead, each of whom would take two kegs, each holding some four gallons, and in a silent file, climb the cliffs, avoiding the country lanes, and pass through the fields to Coombe Cellars, the central clearing house for smuggling. From the pub they were ferried across the river to a kind of bog where the kegs were hidden, payment for this being five shillings. If Mr Rotham didn't receive a signal then he knew the customs men were about and the kegs would be hidden under water, weighed down with sandbags and tied to a raft. They might have to stay down there for weeks. When the coast was clear, at dead of night, the rafts would be dragged ashore and the procession begin. If the weather became stormy before the kegs were landed, they often they broke away and some of the fishermen who had not been included in the smuggling, would seize whatever they could and sell it, although they often watered the brandy before doing so!

The Teign Estuary is a lovely stretch of water to behold but at times it flatters to deceive. In recent years the water has become polluted to such an extent that several people who have been swimming in it have become ill shortly afterwards as a direct result of pollutants in the water. Hopefully something will be done to remedy this totally unacceptable situation or our descendants may well be writing ghost stories about those who died as a result of falling in the Teign—and, judging by the state of the river, they will be the smelliest spooks of all time!

A strong ebb tide carries us down river to its mouth between Teignmouth and Shaldon, which have a few surprises in store.

Once Shaldon was a small village where old sea dogs of all shapes and sizes came to their final anchorage. It consisted originally of two villages, Ringmore and Shaldon, annexed to Teignmouth for urban purposes in 1881. By 1690 Ringmore was a thriving hamlet which included a large house with a tithe barn attached to it, said to have been given to Nell Gwynn by Charles II.

There is also a thatched cottage containing a small circular window which has become known as the Wreckers' Window, presumably because it would once have had a brightly shining lamp burning in it, the light from which would lure ships on to the rocks below. Then the local wreckers would move into action, plundering the remains of the cargo as it smashed against the rocks and, if necessary, murdering any poor souls who managed to survive the wreck.

For any rogues apprehended by the law, there were enough judges ready to dish out the ultimate sentence. High on the hill above Ringmore between Shaldon and Stokein-teignhead is a place called Forches where once a gibbet stood, ready to hang the wreckers, robbers and smugglers.

When Stella Robinson lived in Shaldon she went to the house of Neil and Wyn Hare to nurse the latter during the birth of her third child, knowing nothing of the family. A few days after the birth, Wyn remarked that she was so sorry her mother, who had died a few months before, wouldn't be able to see the new arrival as she had been so fond of babies. A few days later, with the baby in its cot beside her, Stella suddenly saw an elderly lady standing nearby, who smiled as she leant forward to peep at the baby. She was dressed in black with grey stockings, she had a pale and slightly sallow complexion and iron grey hair. She then disappeared as suddenly as she had come. On the corner of the pillow in the cot were five bunches of violets but as Stella bent to pick them up they vanished. She told Wyn what had happened and was informed that the description fitted the baby's late grandmother in every detail. After her death the family had put a wreath of violets on the grave as they were her favourite flowers.

Shaldon is connected to Teignmouth by a road bridge that is over a thousand feet long but can seem much further on foot when a gale force wind blows straight down the estuary! The first Shaldon Bridge was a wooden one and was built in 1827. At that time it was the longest wooden bridge in England, and there was only one longer one in Europe. In 1931 it was replaced and until 1948 wayfarers were obliged to stop at the Teignmouth end to pay a toll. But we don't have this problem today and we can reach Teignmouth with our small change still intact.

Here we have a traditional family resort, albeit on a small scale, which has much to

commend it. Teignmouth's beach has given great joy to millions of visitors down through the years. The bucket and spade brigade have fashioned enough sand castles to repel any invasion force, but how many of the visitors will be aware that these sands have been tampered with by the hand of a ghost? Sir Warwick Tonkin was an important man in Victorian Teignmouth. He had business interests in shipping, was a magistrate and was a friend of Louis Napoleon. He was also a man of talent and vision who, in the early part of the nineteenth century, built a theatre for the townsfolk. However, despite enjoying a successful life something must have played on his mind, some unfulfilled whim perhaps. Within thirty years of his death it is believed that his ghost could be frequently seen on the beach attempting to make ropes out of sand, a chore normally given, in legends, to people guilty of various offences and not a well respected public dignitary like Sir Warwick!

There are dozens of stories of the Devil in Devon—naturally he thinks it is the most beautiful county in England and visits it frequently. One of the most famous and oft told stories is of how the Parson and Clerk rocks between Teignmouth and Dawlish got their names. Legend tells of an elderly priest, keen to become the next Bishop of Exeter, who made haste to reach Dawlish where the present incumbent was dying. Lost on Haldon when a storm blew up, the Devil offered to deliver them safely to Dawlish. But even as the Parson heard the welcome news that the Bishop had died, he and his clerk were swept into the sea, never to be seen again. Two mysterious rocks appeared over night, one bigger than the other, a mile and a half east of Teignmouth—ever since known as the Parson and Clerk.

Whether or not this story has anything to do with the next mention is debatable but high above the town is an ancient ridge called Buckeridge that connected Haldon with the sea. Teignmothians are advised that the ridge should be avoided as its very name is associated with evil—it is supposedly haunted by demons who are thought to ride along it on stormy, dark nights. Although there is a road in the town called Buckeridge Road, residents can sleep soundly as the hauntings are well away from their homes.

Today the town of Teignmouth is a quiet peace-loving haven, but for some strange reason, throughout history, it has been singled out as a target for destruction. Between 890—1020 AD the Danes made a series of determined raids on Teignmouth, the worst raid being in 970 when they slaughtered so many inhabitants that the rocks were said to stream with their blood. Around the year 1340, pirates ransacked the town and burnt down many houses. In July 1690 the French bombarded the defenceless town; whilst the inhabitants made their way to safety, several hundred French sailors landed and made free with their torches, razing to the ground houses and important buildings.

More recently, Teignmouth is regarded by some as being the most heavily bombed settlement, for its size, in England during World War II. From July 1940 to February 1944 some 74 high explosive bombs were rained down onto the town as well as an inordinately high number of incendiary devices. The hospital, fire station, market, library, docks and town hall all suffered direct hits with high explosive bombs. There were 14 machine gun attacks and 88 residents were killed. Out of nearly three thousand buildings in the town only 491 remained unscathed. The railway station was no sanctuary and, despite being in a deep cutting, four trains were machine gunned at various times and all were totally destroyed.

It is more fitting that we should end this journey down the Teign on a happy note and where better than the spot that so many holidaymakers head for come rain or shine. Teignmouth Pier has endured the rigours of the sea for more than a century and is the most distinctive man-made feature of the resort. However it owes its survival to a mixture of

"A South Devon Gem"      Teignmouth Pier

good fortune and to its builders. Arthur Hyde Dendy, a Paigntonian, bought Teignmouth Pier in the early 1870s with the intention of dismantling it and reassembling it at Paignton. Fortunately this proved to be impossible as the piles had been so well anchored to the sea bed that they could not be removed. Instead Dendy renovated the pier, and Paignton didn't lose out either as he built a completely new one there!

We have travelled down the Teign and only revealed some of its history and told only a handful of its tales. The Teign flows ever onward, oblivious to all the machinations of Man. This lovely river is accessible in many locations so we suggest you get out and explore its banks and maybe discover some of your own "Tales of the Teign".